THE
NBA
A HISTORY OF HOOPS

Published by Creative Education
P.O. Box 227, Mankato, Minnesota 56002
Creative Education is an imprint of The Creative Company
www.thecreativecompany.us

Design and production by Christine Vanderbeek
Art direction by Rita Marshall

Printed by Corporate Graphics in the United States of America

Photographs by Corbis (Bettmann), Dreamstime (Munktcu), Getty Images
(Andrew D. Bernstein/NBAE, Otto Greule/Allsport, Walter Iooss Jr./NBAE,
Layne Murdoch/NBAE, Neil Leifer/NBAE, NBA Photo Library/NBAE, Dick
Raphael/NBAE, SM/AIUEO, Rick Stewart, Justin Sullivan, Rocky Widner/NBAE),
iStockphoto (Brandon Laufenberg), US Presswire (Malcolm Emmons)

Library of Congress Cataloging-in-Publication Data
Silverman, Steve.
The story of the Sacramento Kings / by Steve Silverman.
p. cm. — (The NBA: a history of hoops)
Includes index.
Summary: The history of the Sacramento Kings professional
basketball team from its start as the Rochester Royals in 1945
to today, spotlighting the franchise's greatest players and moments.
ISBN 978-1-58341-960-1
1. Sacramento Kings (Basketball team)—History—Juvenile literature.
2. Basketball—California—Sacramento—History—Juvenile literature.
I. Title. II. Series.
GV885.52.S24S32 2010   796.323'640979454—dc22   2009036120

CPSIA: 120109 PO1093

First Edition
2 4 6 8 9 7 5 3 1

Page 3: Forward Chris Webber
Pages 4–5: The Kings' mascot rallying the fans

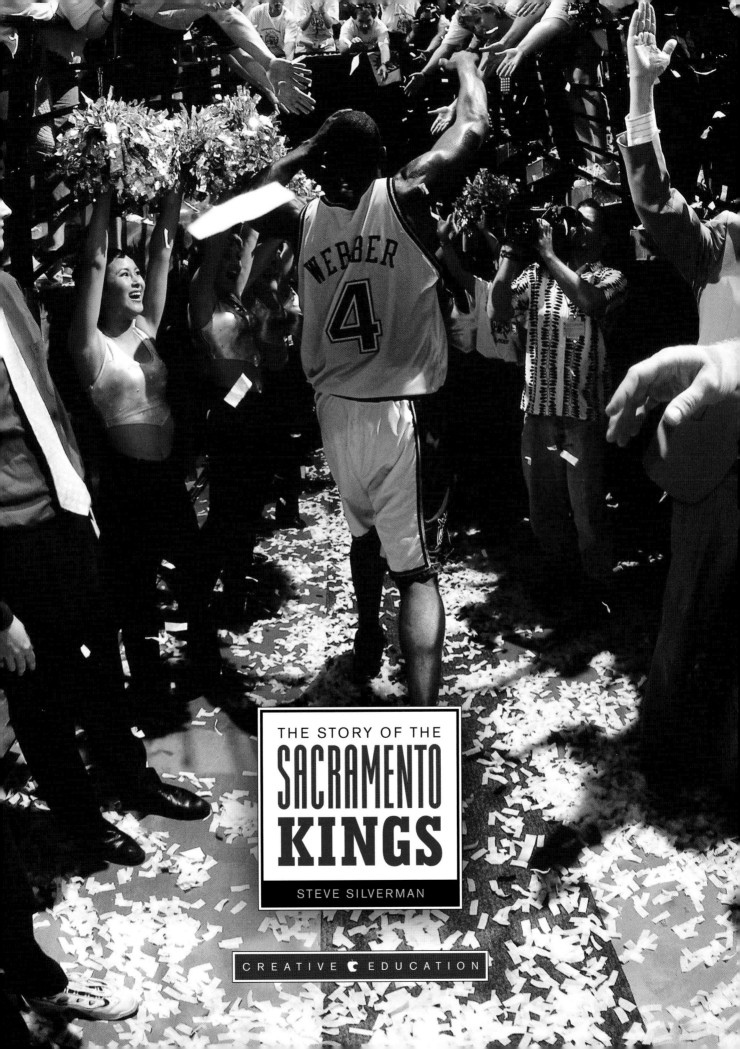

THE STORY OF THE
SACRAMENTO
KINGS

STEVE SILVERMAN

CREATIVE EDUCATION

CONTENTS

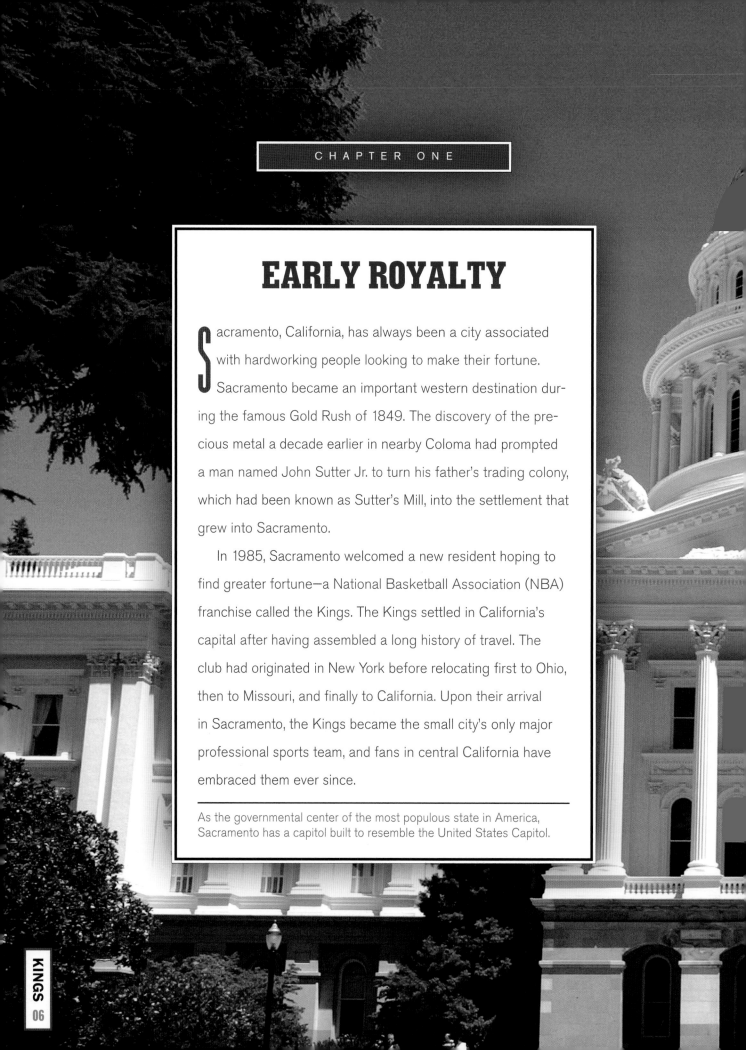

CHAPTER ONE

EARLY ROYALTY

Sacramento, California, has always been a city associated with hardworking people looking to make their fortune. Sacramento became an important western destination during the famous Gold Rush of 1849. The discovery of the precious metal a decade earlier in nearby Coloma had prompted a man named John Sutter Jr. to turn his father's trading colony, which had been known as Sutter's Mill, into the settlement that grew into Sacramento.

In 1985, Sacramento welcomed a new resident hoping to find greater fortune—a National Basketball Association (NBA) franchise called the Kings. The Kings settled in California's capital after having assembled a long history of travel. The club had originated in New York before relocating first to Ohio, then to Missouri, and finally to California. Upon their arrival in Sacramento, the Kings became the small city's only major professional sports team, and fans in central California have embraced them ever since.

As the governmental center of the most populous state in America, Sacramento has a capitol built to resemble the United States Capitol.

The Kings started out far from Sacramento—in Rochester, New York—under a different name and as part of a different league. The Rochester Royals were founded in 1945 and quickly became one of the best teams in the National Basketball League (NBL), winning league championships in both 1946 and 1947. The team was led in those early seasons by such standouts as forward Arnie Risen and guard Bobby Wanzer. Also on the roster was a guard named Otto Graham, who would go on to earn greater fame as a legendary football player for the Cleveland Browns. In 1948, the Royals were among three NBL teams to join the Basketball Association of America (BAA). In 1949, the franchise joined its third league when the BAA and NBL merged to form the NBA.

The NBA's first seasons were fruitful ones for the Royals, who featured terrific guards Bob Davies and Red Holzman. The Royals were title contenders, but winning a championship meant getting past a powerful rival—the Minneapolis Lakers, who featured the league's most dominant big man, 6-foot-10 center George Mikan. Although the Royals boasted as much talent as the Lakers, Rochester could not overcome Mikan's size and strength in the low post, losing to Minneapolis in the 1949 playoffs. "When I started playing with Rochester, it was either us or

Minneapolis that would win it all," Davies later said. "They had the big men, and we had the good little men. That was the difference in a nutshell. It was murder playing against Mikan, because when the Lakers needed two points, he'd get them. George Mikan cost me a lot of money in playoff bonuses and endorsements."

In the 1951 NBA playoffs, Mikan was sidelined by a broken foot, and the Royals capitalized on the opportunity, beating the Lakers three games to one in the Western Division finals. Then, behind balanced scoring from Davies, Risen, and Wanzer, and the all-around contributions of Holzman, the Royals defeated the New York Knicks four games to three to capture the league championship.

The Royals remained a force through the 1952–53 season but could not get past the Lakers again. Then, after two mediocre seasons, new

talent arrived in Rochester in the form of rookie forwards Maurice Stokes and Jack Twyman. The pair, obtained in the 1955 NBA Draft, had great chemistry, but they did not bring immediate team success. The Royals posted losing records in 1955–56 and 1956–57, and attendance at home games in the Rochester Arena plummeted to about 2,000 fans per night. Facing such bleak circumstances, the team's owners decided to seek greener pastures elsewhere, and in 1957, the Royals moved to Cincinnati, Ohio.

COURTSIDE STORIES

THAT CHAMPIONSHIP SEASON

Red Holzman in action in 1950.

THE KINGS FRANCHISE HAS WON ONE NBA CHAMPIONSHIP SINCE IT JOINED THE LEAGUE IN 1949.

That title run came as the Rochester Royals in the 1950–51 season. The Royals beat the Fort Wayne Pistons and the Minneapolis Lakers to advance to the 1951 NBA Finals, where they faced the New York Knicks. The Royals got on a roll early in the series, winning the first two games in Rochester before traveling to New York's Madison Square Garden and beating the Knicks on their home court to take a three-games-to-none lead. The Knicks, however, bounced back with three straight wins to force a pivotal Game 7 in Rochester. The Royals were shaky early on, but the game was tied at 75–75 when Rochester guard Bob Davies drained 2 free throws with 40 seconds remaining. The Royals clinched the game and the title when forward Jack Coleman added a late layup for a 79–75 victory. "We thought we had the title, and then it almost slipped away," said Royals guard Red Holzman (who would later lead the Knicks to two NBA championships as a coach). "But we came through at the end."

ALONG WITH FELLOW FORWARD MAURICE STOKES, JACK TWYMAN WAS ONE OF THE ROCHESTER (AND CINCINNATI) ROYALS' BEST PLAYERS IN THE LATE 1950s..
Drafted in 1955 out of the University of Cincinnati, Twyman paired with Stokes to give the Royals a versatile and high-powered offense. Twyman was a prolific scorer who averaged better than 20 points a game for 4 straight seasons from 1958–59 to 1961–62, using his ability to shake free of defenders with slick low-post moves to consistently earn good looks at the basket. Over the course of his 11-season career with the Royals, he averaged 19.2 points and 6.6 rebounds per game. The scrappy forward also gained distinction as the first player in NBA history to average more than 30 points a game for a season when he netted an average of 31.2 points a night in 1959–60. "It was kind of a dream season for me," Twyman said. "It seemed like I had a big game every time we went out there." After his playing career came to an end, Twyman entered the broadcasting booth as an NBA television analyst.

CHAPTER TWO

THE QUEEN CITY YEARS

The Royals were optimistic as they settled into Cincinnati, a community along the Ohio River nicknamed "The Queen City." Featuring the up-and-coming duo of Stokes and Twyman, the Royals had also obtained powerful young forward Clyde Lovellette in 1957. The Royals finished a mere 33–39, squeaking into the 1958 playoffs, where they lost to the Detroit Pistons in the first round.

The Royals stumbled to a 19–53 mark in 1958–59 and 19–56 the following season, and whispers were heard around the NBA that the team might fold. But Cincinnati's outlook improved dramatically when it obtained guard Oscar Robertson via the 1960 NBA Draft. Team officials had hoped Robertson—who had been a star at the University of Cincinnati—would bring more fans into the Cincinnati Gardens and help the team win a few more games, but they had no idea he would become one of the most dominant players in the game.

Although a solid scorer, Maurice Stokes was best known for his rebounding prowess, grabbing 38 boards in a single game as a rookie.

obertson was a player with no weaknesses. He was a solid ball handler, a fine passer, and a stout defender, and he could either swish shots from the outside or penetrate defenses for soaring dunks or layups. Perhaps most importantly, Robertson played with great confidence even as a rookie—a quality that inspired his teammates on a nightly basis. Robertson, who was nicknamed "The Big O," finished his rookie season with the stunning averages of 30.5 points, 10.1 rebounds, and 9.7 assists per game.

Robertson was even better the following season, averaging 11.4 assists to go along with 30.8 points and 12.5 rebounds per game as the Royals went 43–37. "Don't try to describe the man," said an awestruck Twyman. "You can watch him, you can enjoy him, you can appreciate him, but you can't adequately describe him. It's not any one thing—it's his completeness that amazes you." In the playoffs, however, Cincinnati quickly fell to Detroit.

The Royals got even better in 1962 when they drafted big man Jerry Lucas. Another regional college standout, the former Ohio State University star could play either center or forward, and he developed

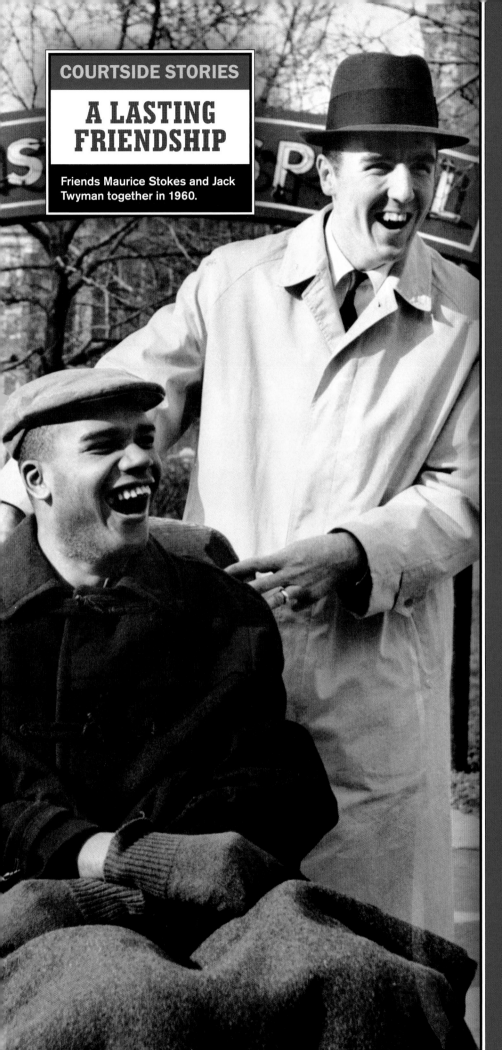

A LASTING FRIENDSHIP

Friends Maurice Stokes and Jack Twyman together in 1960.

WHEN THE ROCHESTER ROYALS MOVED TO CINCINNATI IN 1957, THEY LOOKED LIKE A TEAM READY TO CHALLENGE THE DOMINANT BOSTON CELTICS FOR NBA SUPREMACY. The main reason for optimism in Cincinnati was the stellar one-two punch of forwards Maurice Stokes and Jack Twyman, a couple of superb scorers who could also pass and defend. Stokes had won the 1956 NBA Rookie of the Year award and was widely recognized as one of the league's best players a year later. Sadly, his career was ended—and his life dramatically altered—when he fell to the floor during a game late in the 1957–58 season, hit his head, and suffered a brain injury that ultimately left him paralyzed and confined to a bed. Twyman, who had been friends with Stokes since the two were children, became Stokes's legal guardian and cared for his injured friend until the day he died in 1970. "You'll never know, meet, or read about anybody as courageous as Maurice," said Twyman. "I never heard the man complain in 12 years of lying on his back."

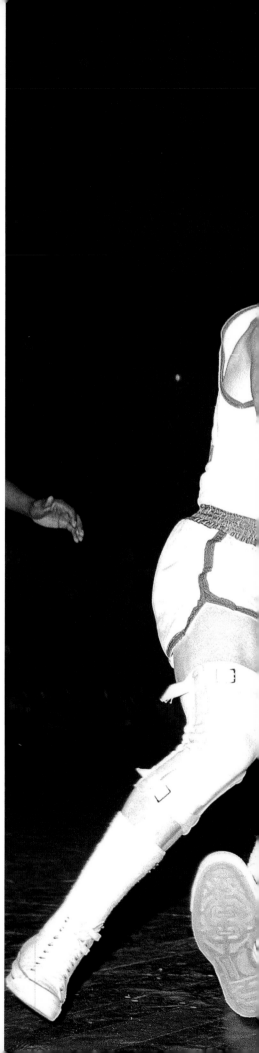

an immediate rapport with Robertson. The two promptly led the Royals to a 42–38 record and another postseason berth. Cincinnati defeated the Syracuse Nationals three games to one in a first-round matchup before losing the Eastern Division finals to the powerful Celtics in a high-scoring, seven-game series.

Despite their playoff struggles, the Royals remained confident of their chances at an NBA title. "We knew we were a good team and had the talent to compete with the best teams in the league," Lucas later explained. "We felt like we had the inside game and the outside game to give a great account of ourselves for 48 minutes. When we were at our best, we caused problems for everyone—Boston, Philadelphia, and the [Los Angeles] Lakers. We thought it was just a matter of time before we would get our turn."

FORMER CHICAGO BULLS GUARD MICHAEL JORDAN IS GENERALLY CONSIDERED TO BE THE GREATEST PLAYER IN NBA HISTORY. But before Jordan came along, Oscar Robertson was the most multitalented player in basketball. "The Big O" had quickness and explosive offensive moves, yet he also dominated on the defensive end with his strength. Robertson essentially invented the concept of the "triple-double" (tallying double digits in three statistical categories in a single game) when he averaged 30.8 points, 12.5 rebounds, and 11.4 assists per game in 1961–62. It is considered a rare achievement for a player to record a triple-double in a game, yet Robertson *averaged* a triple-double every night in that incredible season and came very close to doing it again in the three seasons that followed. As of 2010, no NBA player had ever duplicated that feat. "He obviously was unbelievable, way ahead of his time," said Royals center/forward Jerry Lucas. "There was no more complete player than Oscar." In 1970, the Royals traded Robertson to the Milwaukee Bucks, where he teamed with star center Lew Alcindor to win the 1971 NBA championship.

S till, Cincinnati's postseason frustrations continued the next two
seasons. After enjoying strong regular seasons in 1963–64 and
1964–65, the Royals suffered first-round defeats to Philadelphia and
Boston respectively. While the talent on Cincinnati's roster—headlined
by Robertson, Lucas, guard Adrian Smith, and forward Happy Hairston—
was undeniable, the Royals simply could not attain a position among the
NBA's truly elite.

When the Royals fell to a losing record in 1966–67, Cincinnati gen-
eral manager Joe Axelson brought in former Celtics guard Bob Cousy as
the team's new head coach. Although Cousy had been a Hall of Fame
player, he would find little success as a coach. His hard-driving, demand-
ing personality rubbed Robertson and Lucas the wrong way, and the
Royals soon traded away both stars—Lucas in 1969 and Robertson in
1970. It was rebuilding time in the Queen City.

THE 1962–63 CINCINNATI ROYALS HAD NO FEAR OF THE CELTICS. The NBA's heavyweight franchise from Boston won eight straight league championships between 1959 and 1966 and usually was not seriously challenged. However, when Boston took on Cincinnati in the 1963 Eastern Division finals, the Royals—playing under head coach Jack McMahon—were ready to push the Celtics to the limit. The Royals' top star, guard Oscar Robertson, was at the pinnacle of his game, having averaged 28.3 points per game during the regular season. Although the Royals went only 42–38 during the regular season, they walked into the venerable Boston Garden and served notice that they were ready for a fight by beating the Celtics 135–132 in Game 1. As Royals forwards Jack Twyman and Wayne Embry battled Celtics star center Bill Russell on the boards, the two clubs split the first six games. In the deciding Game 7, however, the Celtics outlasted the scrappy underdogs from Cincinnati, 142–131. "That was a great effort," Robertson said at the series' conclusion. "Nobody gave us a chance against them, and we almost took them down."

THE ROYALS BECAME ONE OF THE MOST EXCITING AND EXPLOSIVE OFFENSIVE TEAMS IN THE NBA WHEN THEY DRAFTED JERRY LUCAS OUT OF OHIO STATE UNIVERSITY IN 1962 TO PLAY ALONGSIDE OSCAR ROBERTSON. Even in the considerable shadow of Robertson, Lucas became a standout. "I never thought of myself as a star," Lucas said. "My only interest was in trying to help the team win." With the Royals, and later with the San Francisco Warriors and New York Knicks, Lucas used his size, strength, and brilliant post moves to become a potent inside scorer who could also step back and notch points with his unique, high-arcing jump shots. A six-time All-Star with the Royals, Lucas put together truly sensational back-to-back seasons in 1967–68 and 1968–69, making more than 50 percent of his shots from the field in both campaigns—a remarkable feat for any player who doesn't exclusively play in the low post. The versatile big man was also a rebounding demon, never averaging fewer than 17.4 boards per game in any of his 6 seasons with the Royals.

CHAPTER THREE

TINY TAKES THE LEAD

The Royals began to develop a new core of stars in 1970 when they drafted a super-quick point guard named Nate Archibald. The Royals also brought in rookie Sam Lacey, a 6-foot-10 center with the size and strength to be a significant presence in the low post. Although Lacey lacked the talent of the elite centers of that era—players such as Kareem Abdul-Jabbar (formerly called Lew Alcindor), Wilt Chamberlain, and Willis Reed—he was strong enough defensively to make his All-Star rivals work hard for their points and rebounds.

By 1972, the Royals were no longer attracting enough Cincinnati fans to be able to remain in Ohio. The team was then sold to a group of businessmen from Kansas City, Missouri, and moved there before the start of the 1972–73 season. In the process, the franchise changed its name to the Kings, since Kansas City's major league baseball team was also called the Royals. Slated to play the bulk of their games in Kansas City, the Kings would also play about 15 games a season in Omaha, Nebraska, in an attempt to widen their fan base.

Sam Lacey was never seen as a superstar, but as a quality scorer, rebounder, passer, and defender, there were few holes in his game.

Although the Kings went just 36–46 in their first Kansas City season, Archibald emerged as one of the most exciting players in the game. The point guard nicknamed "Tiny," who was officially listed at 6-foot-1 yet actually stood no taller than 5-foot-10, was a dynamic scorer who led the NBA in both points and assists that year. Not only did he put up huge numbers, but he did so in entertaining fashion with long, rainbow jumpers and quick cuts to the hoop.

The Kansas City–Omaha Kings dropped the Omaha portion of their name in 1975 and began playing exclusively in Kansas City. As part of their continuing effort to rebuild a talented young lineup, the Kings traded Archibald to the New Jersey Nets in 1976 in exchange for draft picks, which they used to obtain dynamic guards Otis Birdsong and Phil Ford. In addition to working well together on the court, Birdsong and Ford became close friends off of it, and their shared sense of humor helped keep the Kansas City roster relaxed and upbeat. "They're like two peas in a pod," said Cotton Fitzsimmons, who took over as the Kings' coach in 1978. "They're a couple of professional comedians who just happen to play ball in the NBA. They're the guys who keep this team loose, and you have to be loose to play basketball."

Phil Ford reached the peak of his pro career in his third NBA season (1980–81), when he averaged 17.5 points and 8.8 assists per game.

The Kings rose up to win the Western Conference's Midwest Division in 1978–79 but lost to the Phoenix Suns in the first round of the playoffs for the first of two straight years. Two seasons later, the Kings went just 40–42 but hit their stride late in the year. As the postseason began, Fitzsimmons believed his team was ready to play its best ball. "In terms of individual talent, I think you would have to say there is not a lot here," the coach said. "But our club has chemistry. Nobody's going to beat us badly in the playoffs."

Fitzsimmons was right. The Kings beat the favored Portland Trail Blazers two games to one in the first round. They then faced the Suns, the team that had eliminated them from the playoffs the two previous years. Kansas City jumped out to a three-games-to-one lead before the Suns stormed back to tie the series at three wins apiece. Since the decisive Game 7 was in Phoenix, most observers thought the Suns would triumph. But the Kings played their best game of the series, advancing to the Western Conference finals by stunning Phoenix 95–88. The Kings' Cinderella run then ended, though, as the highflying Houston Rockets felled Kansas City in five games to move on to the NBA Finals.

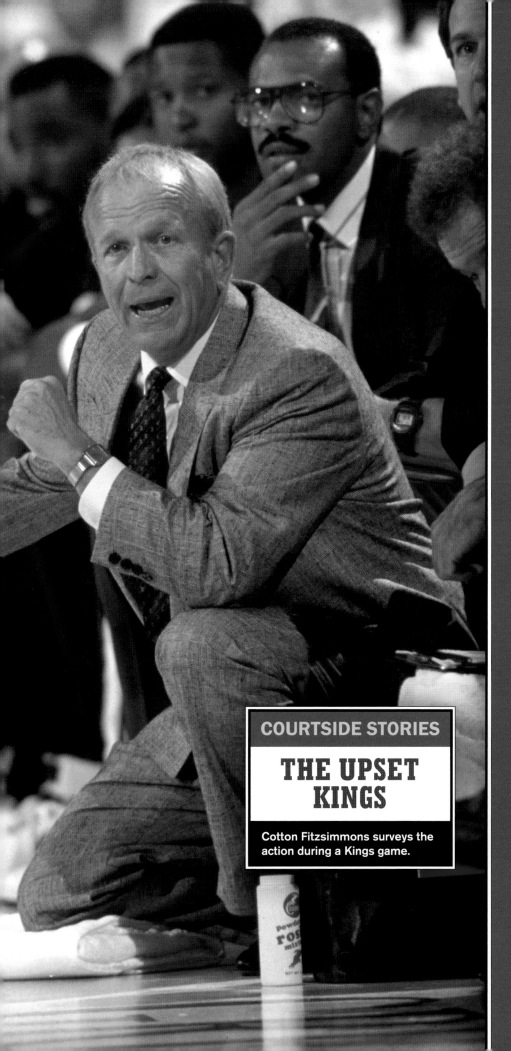

THE UPSET KINGS

Cotton Fitzsimmons surveys the action during a Kings game.

THE KANSAS CITY KINGS WERE A MEDIOCRE TEAM THROUGHOUT THE 1980–81 SEASON. Head coach Cotton Fitzsimmons was a likable leader who preached high-energy defense and the importance of sharing the ball, but his lessons seemed half-learned, as the Kings went just 40–42. That record, though, was good enough to get Kansas City into the playoffs, and Fitzsimmons's players suddenly began to heed their coach's instructions. Behind the outstanding guard duo of Otis Birdsong and Phil Ford, the Kings beat the Trail Blazers in the opening round of the playoffs. That was a surprise, but the Kings pulled off a real shocker in the second round when they beat the powerful Suns, thanks to the clutch shooting of forward Scott Wedman. However, Kansas City's dream of an NBA title then died when the Royals lost to the Rockets in the Western Conference finals. "We thought we might make it all the way to the Finals, but Houston stopped us," said Ford. "But it was a great year all the way around."

POSITION GUARD
HEIGHT 6-FOOT-1
ROYALS / KINGS SEASONS 1970–76

NATE ARCHIBALD

WHEN THE CINCINNATI ROYALS TRADED AWAY JERRY LUCAS IN 1969 AND OSCAR ROBERTSON IN 1970, THEY NEEDED A NEW STAR TO GRAB THE REINS OF THE TEAM AND LEAD. That star came in the unlikely form of Nate "Tiny" Archibald. Although Archibald was short in stature, he had heart and talent in excess. After Archibald averaged 16 points per game

as a rookie, Royals head coach Bob Cousy realized he had a special talent on his hands, and in 1971–72, he made Archibald the focus of the team's offense. The diminutive guard responded by filling up the nets. Zipping around the court with incredible speed, Archibald averaged 28.2 points per game and won over fans not only in Cincinnati but throughout the league. The follow-

ing year, Archibald was perhaps the NBA's best player, leading the league in both scoring (34 points per game) and assists (11.4 per game)—a feat no player had ever achieved before. "I was dedicated to the game," Archibald explained. "I only wanted to get better and help my team improve."

CHAPTER FOUR

WESTWARD HO ... AGAIN

T hat memorable run would turn out to be the greatest, and last, highlight for the Kings in Kansas City. They returned to the playoffs in 1984 but were swept by the Lakers. During a 31–51 campaign the next season, the Kings faced a familiar problem—low fan attendance. And so, in May 1985, the franchise packed up and moved again, heading west to Sacramento.

While the new move would not pay immediate dividends on the court, the Kings were greeted by adoring fans in Sacramento. The team settled into ARCO Arena, which held a mere 10,333 fans. Although that capacity did not reach NBA standards (league arenas were supposed to accommodate at least 15,000 spectators), the Kings received approval to play there since construction on a new, larger arena called ARCO II was ongoing. Although the Kings' new home was small, their new fans compensated by being extra loud. In the club's

Guard Reggie Theus was an explosive scorer, but he was also known for his unselfish passing, ending his NBA career with 6,453 assists.

1985–86 season home opener, Kings guard Larry Drew arrived at the
arena early and was blown away by the enthusiasm of the crowd outside.
"It reminded me of what you see before a college football game," he said.
"It was like the boosters in the parking lot, barbecuing, throwing footballs
around…. People were dressed in tuxedos, and some women were in
evening gowns. They were really getting geared up for their basketball."

The Kings were a high-scoring team in their first year in California's
capital, averaging 108.8 points per game. Led by a pair of sharp-
shooting guards in Eddie Johnson and Reggie Theus, Sacramento
went 37–45 and made the playoffs, only to lose in round one. The Kings
would struggle after that, failing to make the playoffs for the next nine

CALIFORNIA CALLS

The midcourt logo in ARCO Arena.

STABILITY IS ONE THING EVERY SOLID PROFESSIONAL SPORTS TEAM NEEDS, BUT IT'S A COMMODITY THAT ESCAPED THE KINGS FRANCHISE THROUGHOUT MOST OF ITS HISTORY. In 1957, the franchise moved from Rochester to Cincinnati, and in 1972, it relocated to Kansas City. However, the franchise never was able to capture the full support of its home fans in any of the three locations. Fans fell in love with the team in all three cities when it played well, but attendance would evaporate during the difficult times. Prior to the 1985 season, Kings ownership moved the team to Sacramento. A city of fewer than 400,000 people at the time, Sacramento had no other big-time sports franchise, and the capital city welcomed the club enthusiastically. The Kings opened their run in Sacramento before a full house on October 25, 1985, and the fans were ecstatic, even though the team dropped a 108–104 decision to the Los Angeles Clippers. Not only did fans fill the 10,333-seat ARCO Arena on a nightly basis, they did it with passion. "Those fans were crazy," recalled Kings guard Reggie Theus. "They loved us, and they were loud every night."

MITCH RICHMOND WAS ALREADY A FULL-FLEDGED NBA STAR BY THE TIME HE ARRIVED IN SACRAMENTO VIA TRADE IN 1991. The guard had excelled with the fast-moving and high-scoring Golden State Warriors, but many fans thought Richmond's play would decline in Sacramento, where talent was scarce and the team had long struggled. Not only did Richmond not regress, he raised his level of play significantly as he was anointed the Kings' leader. Richmond was a lethal scorer with one of the most accurate jump shots the NBA had ever seen, and he led Sacramento in scoring in each of his 7 seasons there, making the All-Star Game every year but 1 and never averaging fewer than 21.9 points per game. For many years, he was the lone bright spot for a Kings team that lost often and was frequently blown out. "You're talking about a guy who persevered through some tough times in Sacramento," Kings team president Geoff Petrie said. "He was a great, great player and a great competitor— one for the ages."

INTRODUCING...

MITCH RICHMOND

POSITION GUARD
HEIGHT 6-FOOT-5
KINGS SEASONS 1991–98

seasons. Even the coaching leadership of former NBA greats Bill Russell and Willis Reed and the efforts of such players as center Joe Kleine, swingman Harold Pressley, and guard Danny Ainge could not get the team over the hump.

In the early 1990s, the Kings suited up such quality players as forwards Antoine Carr, Wayman Tisdale, and Lionel Simmons, and long-range-bombing guard Mitch Richmond. Still, Sacramento remained a losing club. The team hit several low points during the 1990–91 season. The Kings scored just 59 points in a 101–59 loss to the Charlotte Hornets, the lowest output by an NBA team since 1955. They also closed the season with 37 straight road losses, setting a new NBA record.

Things finally started to turn around for the Kings in 1994–95, when they finished 39–43. Sacramento matched that mark the following season and even made the playoffs. The franchise's outlook brightened further when brothers Joe and Gavin Maloof, a pair of wealthy hotel moguls, bought the team in 1997–98. The Kings put together a winning record the following year, going 27–23 in a season shortened by a labor dispute between NBA owners and players.

In 1998, the Kings overhauled their roster, trading Richmond to the Washington Wizards for powerful forward Chris Webber, drafting an exciting passing point guard named Jason Williams, and picking up veteran center Vlade Divac as a free agent. Playing with greater chemistry and a new sense of flair, the new-look Kings enjoyed a winning season in 1999–2000 and really came into their own in 2000–01, recording a 55–27 record that was the fourth-best in the NBA. "We had something going, there's no doubt about that," Webber later said. "We were in the process of becoming one of the most competitive teams in the league, and other teams had a hard time defending us. We had a lot of offensive options, and our confidence was growing. We liked playing together and thought it would be just a matter of time as to when we got our championship."

Sacramento's 2001–02 season was one to remember, as the Kings streaked to a stunning 61–21 record. With Webber scoring 24.5 points per game, swingman Peja Stojakovic netting another 21.2 per night, and point guard Mike Bibby's slick ball handling and passing pacing the offense, the Kings boasted one of the most versatile attacks in the NBA. In the playoffs, the Kings cruised past the Utah Jazz and Dallas Mavericks in the first two rounds, then met the powerful Lakers in the Western Conference finals. Although Sacramento seized a three-games-to-two lead in the series with a 92–91 victory in Game 5, it could not seal the deal. The Lakers stormed back to win the next two games, concluding what was one of the most physical and intense battles in recent NBA playoffs history.

Unfortunately, the Kings had reached their peak. The core of Sacramento's team remained intact through the 2004–05 season, but

INTRODUCING...

CHRIS WEBBER

POSITION FORWARD
HEIGHT 6-FOOT-9
KINGS SEASONS 1998–2005

CHRIS WEBBER HAD MADE A NAME FOR HIMSELF AS A MEMBER OF THE "FAB FIVE" (A GROUP OF FIVE OUTSTANDING FRESHMEN) AT THE UNIVERSITY OF MICHIGAN AND AS A SOLID PLAYER WITH THE WARRIORS AND WASHINGTON BULLETS BEFORE BEING TRADED TO THE KINGS. Initially, Webber was not interested in reporting to Sacramento because he didn't want to go to such a small city and to a team that had Sacramento's losing history. Webber warmed to the city, though, as the franchise added such players as center Vlade Divac. The union benefited both sides. The Kings improved dramatically, and Webber's career took off. The brawny forward earned All-Star status for 5 straight seasons, and in 2000–01, he averaged a career-best 27.1 points per game. Webber was also a top-tier rebounder, and Kings head coach Rick Adelman made sure the team took advantage of his slick passing skills by running much of the offense through him.

"It was a great and special time," Webber later said of his Sacramento seasons. "We didn't get that title, but it was still an awesome team."

THE KINGS' 2001–02 SEASON WAS ONE OF THE GREATEST IN FRANCHISE HISTORY. At the start of the year, Sacramento switched point guards by trading Jason Williams to the Vancouver Grizzlies for Mike Bibby, a move that helped spark the team to a franchise-best 61–21 record and had the Kings and their fans dreaming about an NBA championship. After Bibby, star forward Chris Webber, and the rest of the Kings won two playoff series, they met the Lakers in the Western Conference finals, a bruising, back-and-forth series that came down to a deciding Game 7 played in Sacramento. In the fourth quarter, Bibby nailed two free throws to tie the game 100–100 and send it into overtime. The extra session belonged to the Lakers, though, as center Shaquille O'Neal and his teammates ran away to a 112–106 win. With the bitter defeat, the Kings became the first NBA team in 20 years to lose a Game 7 playoff contest at home. "It hurts. It really hurts big," Bibby said. "We should have closed it out when we had the opportunity."

COURTSIDE STORIES

CLOSE BUT NO CIGAR

Vlade Divac tips a shot in versus the Lakers in the 2002 playoffs.

the Kings could not advance past the second round of the playoffs. In 2005, Webber left town, and Sacramento tried to fill the void by bringing in tough forward Ron Artest, the 2004 NBA Defensive Player of the Year. The fiery forward's addition, though, was not enough to prevent Sacramento from posting mediocre records the next three seasons. In 2006–07, the Kings missed the playoffs for the first time in nine years.

After another losing campaign in 2007–08, Sacramento set about rebuilding, adding such players as rookie forward Jason Thompson, who impressed Sacramento scouts with his hustle and touch around the basket. "I saw quite a bit of his tape, and I had talked to the coaching staff," said Artest. "I knew he was going to be a good player. So I called him to welcome him aboard and tell him what we had going on here. I thought we were going to win a championship and I think I convinced him because he was agreeing with me."

Artest, though, would not be around for any championship runs, as the Kings soon traded him to Houston in a deal that brought veteran point guard Bobby Jackson and forward Donte Green to Sacramento. The move did little to boost the Kings, who became one of the worst

teams in the league in 2008–09. Young guard Kevin Martin poured in points in bunches, and veteran center Brad Miller worked the boards hard, yet the Kings were frequently thumped during a 17–65 season. Fortunately, after this painful season, the Kings struck gold in the 2009 NBA Draft, nabbing shooting guard Tyreke Evans, who promptly led the club with 20.1 points per game to earn the 2010 NBA Rookie of the Year award. Sacramento missed the playoffs again, but new coach Paul Westphal liked the team's young core of Evans, Thompson, and guard Beno Udrih. "The journey is just beginning," Westphal said. "We added eight more wins and added some players we can build around, so by any measure, there was improvement."

It has been a long time since the Kings franchise celebrated an NBA championship—three relocations, one name change, and about six decades ago. Yet since that 1950–51 Rochester Royals team won it all, the Royals/Kings have entertained fans in Cincinnati, Kansas City, Omaha, and Sacramento with some of the premier stars in the league. As the always vocal Sacramento faithful continue to throw their support behind the Kings, it may be only a matter of time before Sacramento purple is the color of an NBA champion.

Although just a rookie, Tyreke Evans assumed a leadership role for the Kings in 2009–10, especially after fellow guard Kevin Martin (with ball, pages 46–47) was traded away in the middle of the season.

INDEX